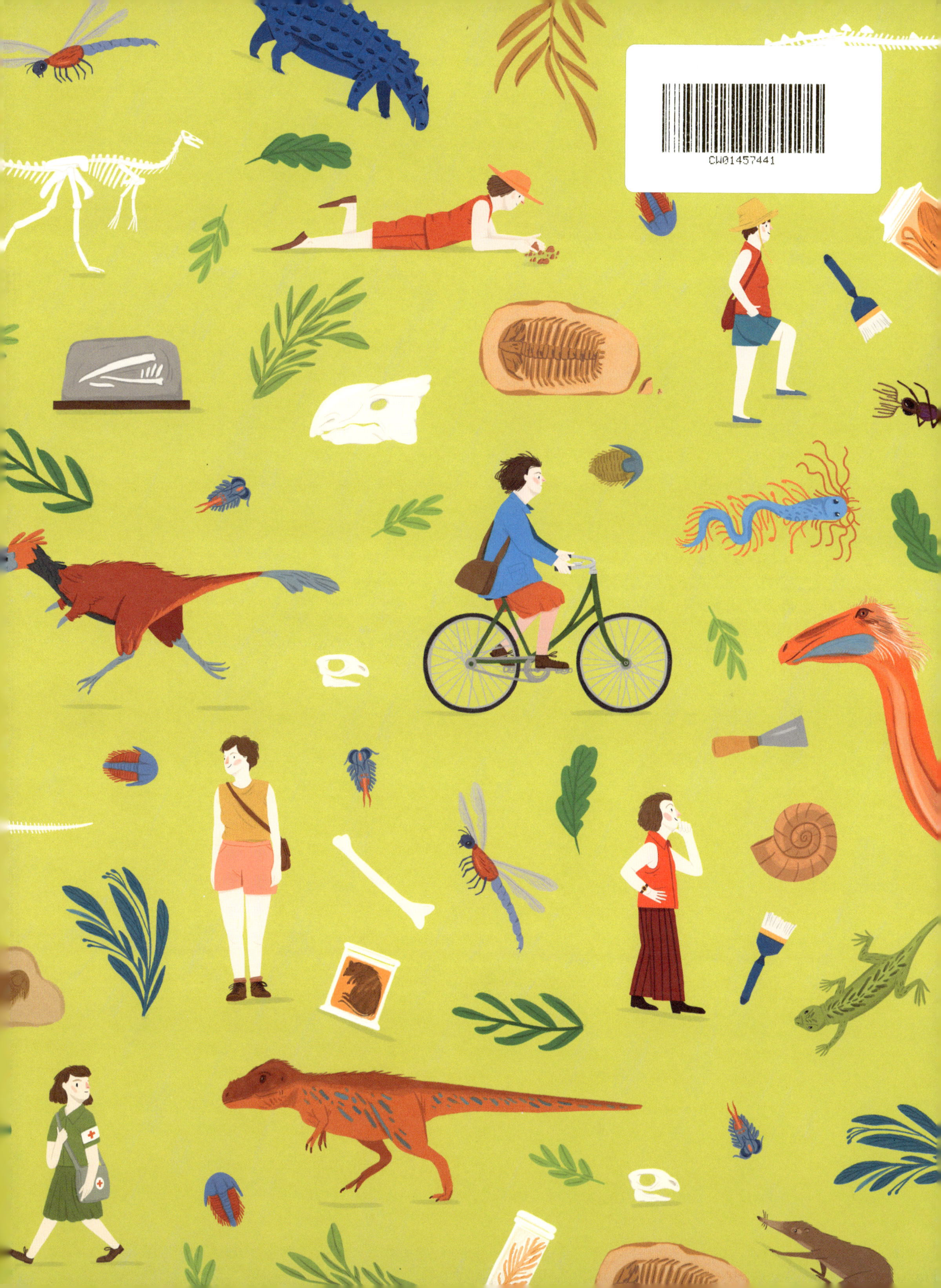

To the children of conflict. — N.C.

For Tymon and Ignacy. — O.P.

WITH THANKS TO...

Professor Magda Borsuk-Białynicka, for her recollections of the Mongolian expeditions; Rafał Brodacki of the Warsaw Uprising Museum for his comments on the book; Professor Jarosław Stolarski, Head of the Institute of Palaeobiology, Polish Academy of Sciences, and Dr Bolortsetseg Minjin, Director of the Institute for the Study of Mongolian Dinosaurs, for their invaluable help verifying details in the text; Professor Phil Cox, Dr Elsa Panciroli and Dr Pam Gill for double checking the science; Professor Anjali Goswami and Dr Tori Herridge for their encouragement; and Dr Krzysztof Koza and Dr Andrzej Wolniewicz for their help at the early stages of this project. Sophie Hallam and Laura Hall for their unwavering belief and optimism in this book. Finally, thanks to Mariusz and Zosia Jaworowski — the family of Zofia Kielan-Jaworowska — for their help detailing Zofia's life and granting us permission to tell her story.

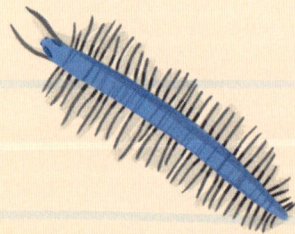

A TEMPLAR BOOK

First published in the UK in 2025 by Templar Books, an imprint of Bonnier Books UK 5th Floor, HYLO, 105 Bunhill Row, London, EC1Y 8LZ The authorised representative in the EEA is Bonnier Books UK (Ireland) Limited. Registered office address: Floor 3, Block 3, Miesian Plaza, Dublin 2, D02 Y754, Ireland compliance@bonnierbooks.ie

Text copyright © 2025 by Dr Nick Crumpton Illustration copyright © 2025 by Ola Płocińska Design copyright © 2025 by Templar Books

10 9 8 7 6 5 4 3 2 1

ISBN 978-1-80078-665-3

Edited by Sophie Hallam (aka Zosia)
Designed by Laura Hall
Production by Neil Randles

Printed in China

A TEMPLAR BOOK NO. 2408

templar books

DINOSAUR DESERT

Written by
DR NICK CRUMPTON

Illustrated by
OLA PŁOCIŃSKA

Nemegtosaurus

CONTENTS

Zofia's first fossil!

PART ONE

	8
Life on Earth	10
From one war to another	12
Resistance fighters	14
My name is Zofia Kielan	16
Warsaw Uprising and escape	18
Rebuilding lives	

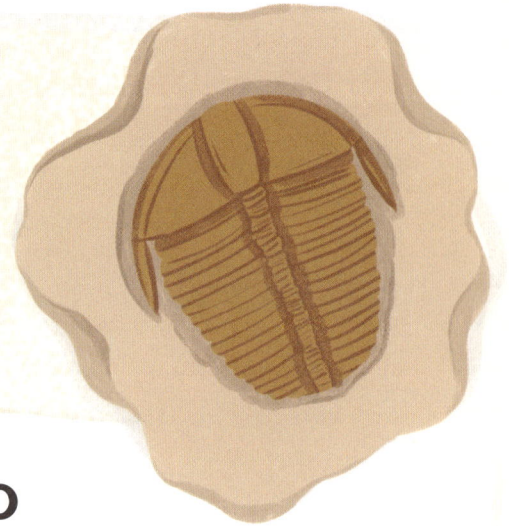

PART TWO

Studying fossils	20
Discovering the Gobi Desert	22
Becoming a palaeontologist	24
Travels to Mongolia	26
A palaeontology kit list	28
Preparing for the trip	30

Ammonite

Megazostrodon

Archaeopteryx

PALAEOZOIC (521–250 MYA)

MESOZOIC (250–66 MYA)

PART THREE

Arrival in Mongolia 32

Meet the team 34

A day in the life of the desert camp 35

Scorpians, spiders and sandstorms 38

Unearthing something huge 40

Excavating fossils 42

Some exciting finds 44

The 'horrible hand' 46

The greatest mystery yet 48

↑ Kennalestes skull

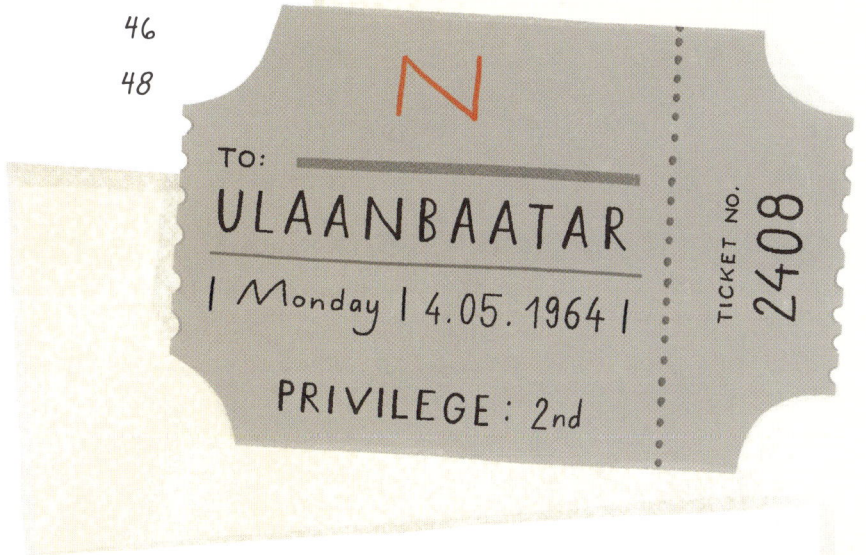

TO: _____
ULAANBAATAR
| Monday | 4.05.1964 |
PRIVILEGE: 2nd
TICKET NO. 2408

ADMITS ONE
Chorzów
DINOSAUR PARK

PART FOUR

Dinosaurs on display 50

The pursuit of mammals 52

Surviving in the Cretaceous 54

The journey ends 56

Dinosaur Valley 58

Science across borders 60

Tyrannosaurus rex

Mammoth

Zofia Kielan-Jaworowska 1925–2015

CENOZOIC (66 MYA–now)   MYA = million years ago

The sun burns steadily overhead, as it always
has and always will. Below the vast blue sky,
a *Parvicursor* fills its belly full of delicious termites
while a *Catopsbaatar* scurries home to its mate.

Parvicursor

Catopsbaatar

Until a cosmic wanderer, a meteorite from outer space, extinguished three-quarters of Earth's species...

Only a few survived and evolved.

Gradually, life returned to old places in new shapes...

Until, millions of years later, the world changed once more.

Nr. 124 | Cena numeru: **25 gr.** | # KURIER

FROM ONE WAR TO ANOTHER

A NEW GERMAN CHANCELLOR

The year is 1933 and Adolf Hitler has risen to power in Germany. His speeches, his writings, his films – all his propaganda has convinced Germans that they are the rightful rulers of Europe. And that they should 'take back' what they lost following World War I.

DEVASTATING LOSS: World War I (1914 –1918) was one of the deadliest global wars in history. 40 million people died. It was fought between the Entente Powers (France, the United Kingdom, Russia, the United States, Italy and Japan, among others) and the Central Powers (Germany, Austria-Hungary, the Ottoman Empire and Bulgaria).

1,2 MILLIARDEN FÜR FÜRSTEN

JOBS NEEDED: Germany and the Central Powers had been defeated in this brutal and devastating war. In 1919, the Treaty of Versailles made Germany pay for the war, reduce its army and lose territory. Soon after, the Great Depression of the 1930s meant that millions were out of work and the country faced starvation and misery.

WARSZAWSKI

Many Germans quickly fell under the spell of the Nazi party. Hitler promised to bring Germany back to greatness by giving people jobs and ridding the country of anyone 'who was not like them'. To the Nazis, this meant People of Colour, Roma and Sinti people, men who loved men, women who loved women, people from Slavic nations like Poland and Russia and, above all else, people of the Jewish faith.

This hatred was built on hundreds of years of anti-semitic lies, and Hitler used it to unite people to vote him into power. When they made him leader of Germany, he did everything he could to destroy the Jewish people...

HITLER INVADES POLAND

But ruling over Germany was not enough for Hitler, who wanted complete control over Europe. So, in 1939, Nazi Germany invaded Poland and set in motion a chain reaction that eventually pitted the United Kingdom, the United States of America, France, Belgium, Greece and many other countries against the Nazis and their allies. Hitler's war destroyed families, crushed cities, and ended the lives of over 80 million people.

1933

Hitler appointed Chancellor of Germany.

Boycott of Jewish businesses, and Jewish people no longer allowed jobs at universities.

Public burning of books written by Jews.

Concentration camps are built.

~

1935

The Nuremberg Laws: Jewish people no longer considered German citizens; cannot marry non-Jewish people or fly the German flag.

~

1938

Kristallnacht (Night of Broken Glass): 200 synagogues destroyed; 7,500 Jewish shops looted; 30,000 Jewish people sent to concentration camps.

All Jewish pupils expelled from German schools.

Germany expands its power by gaining territory in Czechoslovakia and Austria.

~

1939

Germany advances into Prague, and invades Poland on 1 September. France and United Kingdom declare war on Germany. World War II begins.

Europe – and almost the whole world – was now at war, ever since Nazi soldiers had marched into Poland: the first step in their rampage of invasion.

Warsaw, Poland's capital city, had been overtaken in just three weeks, and its people trapped. Almost half a million Jews were forced to live in a small neighbourhood – the Warsaw Ghetto – in terrible conditions. Many of those trapped fought back in the Warsaw Ghetto Uprising, a brave defiance against the Nazis despite overwhelming odds. But to no avail. Many thousands died on the streets of their city or were deported to concentration camps.

And now, Warsaw was on its knees. The Nazis had taken control. Its goal: the complete destruction of the Polish people and their culture. Day by day, Polish people were sentenced to death on the streets. Families were driven from their homes, and imprisoned in forced labour or concentration camps. Museums, libraries and theatres were closed or destroyed, and Polish children were banned from attending school.

But the Polish people would not give up easily. For years, ordinary people – shopkeepers, bankers, teachers and artists – secretly did what they could to resist the Nazis. An underground government, over one hundred secret societies, and an invisible army were sabotaging trains carrying goods and soldiers, freeing captives from Nazi prisons, blowing up bridges and fighting against their occupiers in the streets.

And somewhere in the chaos of the once beautiful city was Zofia. A girl whose life, like all those around her, had been paused while the world was at war.

My name is Zofia Kielan...

I was born in 1925 in Sokołów Podlaski. These are my parents Franciszek and Maria, and my sister Krystyna.

Move to Warsaw

In 1934, my dad got a job in Warsaw so we all moved to a district called Żoliborz. I was very happy growing up there. I loved to read (sometimes even at parties) and often squabbled with Krystyna...

Fun at scout camp

Krystyna and I spent our summer holidays as part of the Polish Scouting Movement. We loved spending time outdoors, camping, and learning how to start fires!

Poland is invaded

When the Nazis stormed my city in 1939, I was only 14. My world was turned upside down.

ZHP

Polish resistance

I was proud to serve as a medic as part of the Polish resistance. I was in the Grey Ranks and Krystyna joined 'Help to the Soldiers'. We were on the front line of battles being waged in our city.

Secret studies

We weren't allowed to go to school but we kept on with our studies in secret, hidden in people's houses. If we had been discovered, we would have been shot! In my secret classes, reading my ancient biology textbook, I could escape the bullets and soldiers. I forgot the danger and the fear and travelled in my mind to worlds before dictators, before nations, before wars.

Jana joins the family

In 1941, I was so happy because Jana Prot joined our class and we became great friends. But then one day, Jana was separated from her family and had to leave her home. Could it be because her father was Jewish? And an important factory director from Pionki? There was no question of what we should do: Jana came to live with us. My parents were so scared because keeping her safe was a crime in the eyes of the Nazis.

The war in Europe changed in 1944. Soldiers from all over the world, intent on stopping the Nazis, landed in France on 6 June and began a mission to save the continent from oppression, sending a wave of hope across Europe.

D-Day was the largest seaborne invasion in history and began the liberation of France (and later Western Europe).

In Warsaw, Polish people took up their weapons and began a final fight for their home. Zofia and Jana stopped studying and worked as medics, helping the wounded through the shattered city streets.

They had hoped to fight for just a few days until the forces of the Soviets came to help them. But the Polish people fought in the streets for more than two brutal months.

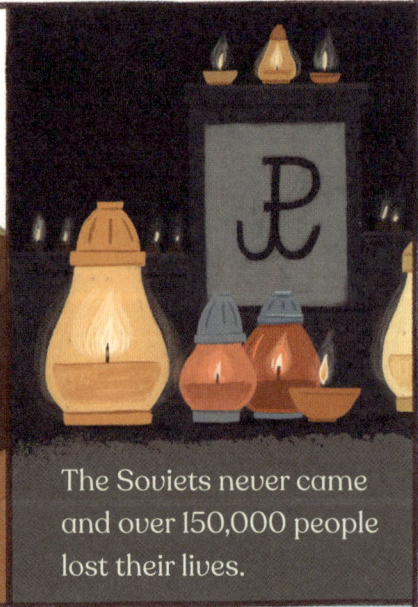

The Soviets never came and over 150,000 people lost their lives.

The Warsaw Uprising had ultimately failed and the Nazis ordered the entire city to be emptied. Hundreds of thousands of people, including Zofia, her mother and Jana, were moved to a transit station in Pruszków, where they were either sent to death camps or to other parts of Nazi-controlled Poland.

Zofia, as a healthy young woman, was sent to work in a camp, but by chance a doctor working in Pruszków recognised her and gave her a fake medical certificate to convince the Nazis she was carrying the terrible disease tuberculosis.

Jana pretended to be pregnant, tying a pillow around her waist, and so the two girls, along with Zofia's mother, were sent away on board an open-topped train carriage usually used to move cattle.

Under the cover of a rainstorm, Zofia, her mother and Jana escaped, jumping over the wagon's sides and hiding with a railway worker friendly to the resistance.

They boiled their clothes to kill the lice from the journey, and hid with others who had escaped from the Nazi trains until Zofia's father tracked them down.

Together, at last, although far from their home, they were finally safe.

By 1945, the terrible war was finally over. After five years of oppression, Germany and the Axis powers had been defeated.

As the Nazis began to lose the war, they had scattered, running from the cities they had captured. But Warsaw was different. Hitler was determined to destroy the city following the Warsaw Uprising. So, at the end of 1944, as the Nazis' defeat across Europe seemed certain, they left the already wounded city, but then turned their weapons back on it.

They set fire to churches and smashed down schools, demolished museums and stole from art galleries. They shot and crushed, tore and toppled and in just a few months, Warsaw, Zofia's beautiful home, was almost wiped from the face of the Earth.

Zofia walked back to the remains of her city, but in Żoliborz she found her beautiful home had been destroyed. Almost nothing had survived except, incredibly, her bicycle.

She pedalled through the ghostly city. Street after street lay ruined but, to her surprise, she discovered that the Museum of Zoology was still – just about – standing.

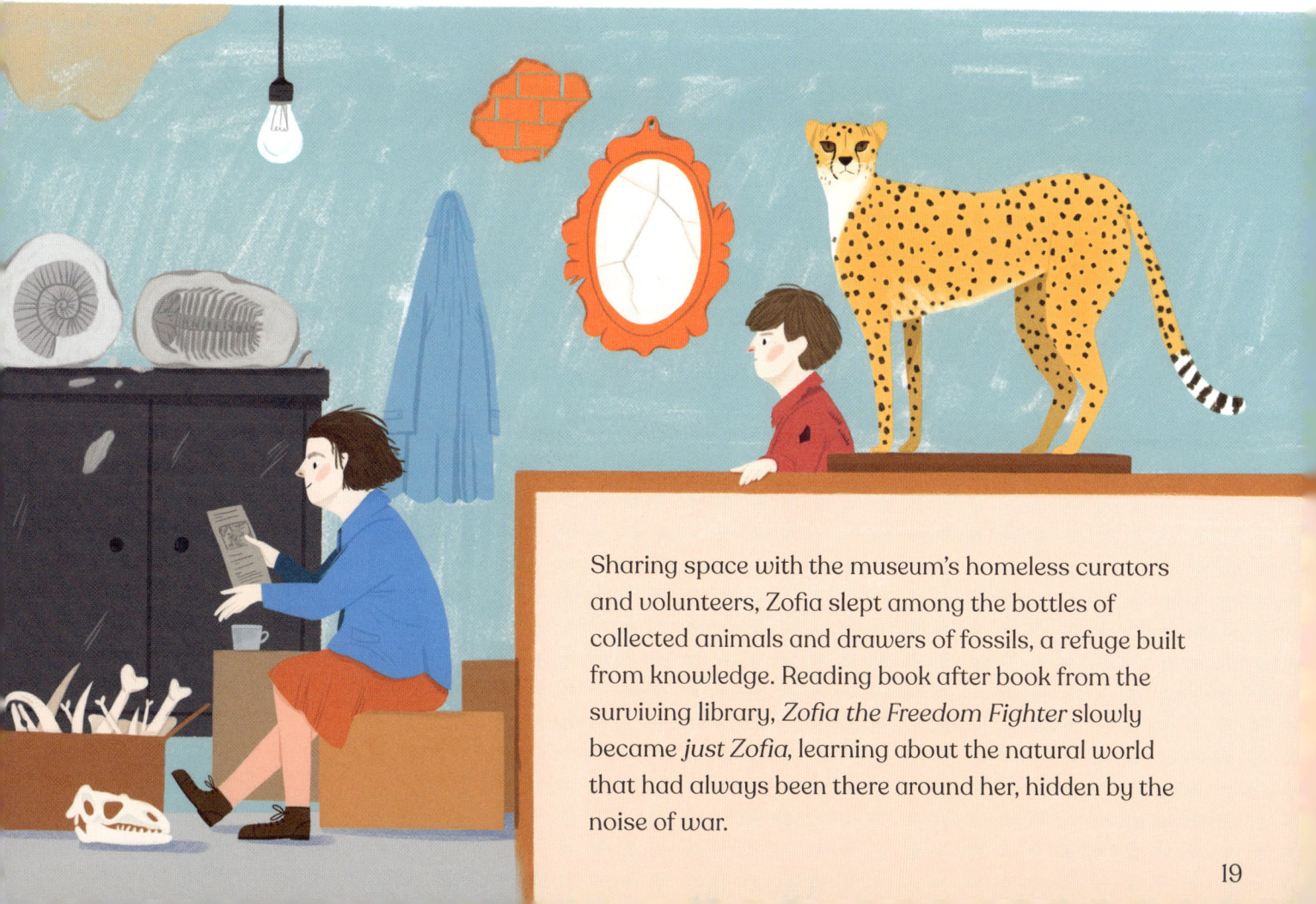

Sharing space with the museum's homeless curators and volunteers, Zofia slept among the bottles of collected animals and drawers of fossils, a refuge built from knowledge. Reading book after book from the surviving library, *Zofia the Freedom Fighter* slowly became *just Zofia*, learning about the natural world that had always been there around her, hidden by the noise of war.

Zofia's time spent among the curators and specimens of the museum
had convinced her: she would study biology at her city's university.
But the university had barely any buildings still standing:
its classrooms had been levelled, its libraries lay in ruins.

Instead, Zofia was taught
wherever her teachers could find
space. It was in one such place,
in the apartment of Professor
Kozłowski on Wilcza Street,
where her life changed forever.

Professor Kozłowski stood behind his table and drew on his blackboard, speaking quickly as he taught Zofia's small class about the countless species that had lived throughout the history of life on Earth.

And it was in this room, in this small apartment, that Zofia learned about the daring expeditions of Roy Chapman Andrews, 20 years ago.

ZALAMBDALESTES

MONGOLIA

This American palaeontologist and his team had been on a mission to find human fossils but had, miraculously, found dinosaur bones instead!

Zofia learned about the dangers of working in the desert, about the wonderful people they had encountered, and the dinosaur eggs and mammal skulls they had prised from the sandy rocks of Bayn Dzak.

Zofia was *entranced.*

Adasaurus

Where the Gobi Desert now stretched – endless, barren, inhospitable – there had once been a bustling ancient shoreline. In her mind, Zofia waded in freshwater rivers and explored the conifer forests, rich with the scents of the Earth's first flowers. The humid air was thick with the chatter of insects overhead, while the shadows of dinosaurs passed between the trees and her mammal ancestors scampered underfoot.

Zalambdalestes

Alioramus

Saurolophus

Deltatheridium

Where there was nothing, there had once been everything.

Following the war, travel was near impossible so Zofia started to look at ancient animals she could find far closer to home.

As Poland began its next difficult chapter, Zofia became a palaeontologist and spent the next 14 years in her home country, climbing the heights of the Holy Cross Mountains – and travelling 360 million years back in time to the Devonian period.

This was the age of huge armoured fish, of the first early plants on land, and the very beginnings of the backboned animals that would eventually take slippery steps up out of the water.

Back then, most of what is now Poland was underwater, so the fossils Zofia found had all settled at the bottom of an ancient ocean.

Zofia found and studied trilobites – hard-shelled, aquatic relatives of insects and crabs – that had once thrived in this underwater world. By the Devonian period, these ancient creatures had existed on Earth for over 100 million years. Their bodies, sometimes elegant, often gnarled or covered in bumps, reflected countless adaptations to their marine habitats.

After becoming an expert on these ancient invertebrates, Zofia began excavating the fossils of polychaete worms. These creatures had once burrowed through the long-lost seabed, leaving behind only their tiny jaws, preserved in the rocks she carefully dissolved in acid.

Zofia was learning the history of the Earth and how to read the secret stories held in the smallest of fossils.

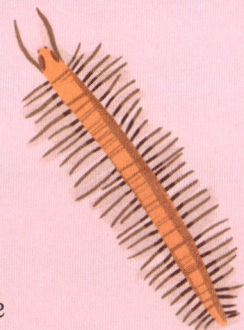

Zofia longed to visit museums in other countries, to see famous fossils with her own eyes. But travelling outside Poland was not easy.

Her country had changed again since the end of the war, and even had a new name: the Polish People's Republic. But this was a 'satellite state', controlled by the Soviets – the same politicians who had stolen Polish land and abandoned the Polish people during the Warsaw Uprising.

2K

4K

UNION OF SOVIET

Moscow

London

Paris

East Germany

Warsaw

West Germany

Naples

The Soviets were powerful, spreading their ideas and beliefs across Eastern Europe, cutting themselves off from America and the rest of Europe to the west. This was known as the Iron Curtain. Although there was no fighting between these two groups of nations, the world was locked in a cold war with both sides distrusting the other.

After the war, Germany was divided among the Allied forces — West Germany was controlled by the USA, UK and France, while East Germany was under Soviet control. In 1961, the Berlin Wall was built, physically separating East Germany from West Germany — breaking up families, creating further divides.

The Iron Curtain was an invisible boundary separating the East and West.

Zofia did manage to travel to Western Europe but it was much easier to visit other Soviet countries. Her bosses were keen to show off Soviet science to the world, and she saw her chance for adventure! Mongolia – another Soviet satellite state – was the country Zofia had longed to visit for so long.

Zofia didn't think that anyone would give her the money to mount an expedition to the Gobi Desert. After all, she was an expert in trilobites and ancient worms, not dinosaurs. But, thanks to her talent for finding fossils and her knowledge of where the Americans had (and had not) dug in the 1930s, she was given the funds to visit Mongolia and work with scientists there – tasked with bringing back to Warsaw the city's first dinosaurs.

SOCIALIST REPUBLICS (USSR)

Zofia thought of herself as a young woman studying in Professor Kozłowski's apartment and could barely believe it: she would soon be sitting on a plane to Mongolia's capital city, Ulaanbaatar.

Ulaanbaatar

01.08.64
WARSAW

Polish Airline

FLIGHT NR
157

But first, there was a lot to do. Zofia assembled a small band of fellow scientists who would arrive by train – just before her – in Mongolia in the spring of 1964.

Throughout the winter in Warsaw, they prepared for their journey. They were going to have to take more than just their passports and sunglasses. Zofia's team crammed everything into wooden crates, hammered them shut, and sent them about 7,000km over land by train.

Everything they would need would be waiting for them when they arrived.

THEY WOULD NEED:

* pens and ink for drawing and typewriters for writing up their findings

* 40 hammers, 20 pickaxes, 33 spades, 100 chisels, 50 paint brushes and 1 hand pulley for excavation

* 2 tonnes of plaster for protecting any bones they found

* wood, nails, screws and tools for building crates to transport fossils

* 120 litres of liquid polystyrene and 200 square metres of corrugated cardboard for packing fossils

* 150 square metres of canvas

* 14,000 litres of petrol, and a repair kit for their enormous trucks

* food, knives, forks, spoons, and a field kitchen for the whole team over four months

* tents, sleeping bags, blow-up matresses

* light clothes for the blistering heat of the day, and warm layers for the freezing desert nights

* a medicine chest

* flashlights and candles

29

Zofia knew that they could bring all the finest equipment, the newest tools and the biggest trucks, but the most important thing they could take with them couldn't be packed in a box. If she didn't understand the country she was visiting, they would have no hope of finding their way out of the airport, let alone finding fossils. So, in the months before she left, Zofia invited two of Mongolia's finest palaeontologists, Naidan Dovchin and Demberel Dashzeveg, to brave the Polish winter with her in Warsaw.

They spoke together for days about their country, Mongolia, about its history – not only of dinosaurs, but of the ancient Xiongnu empire, Buddhist monks and Chingis Khaan.

MONGOLIA

Zofia learned how to read Mongolian maps and speak a few phrases in their language. They taught her about *gers* – the traditional homes of Mongolia's nomadic people – which were strong enough to withstand sandstorms but light enough to be carried from valley to valley. They told her about the traditional deel clothes still worn on the steppe and of *heviin boov* cookies that crumbled sweetly on the tongue. They read microfilms about dinosaur fossils discovered in the 1920s and planned their trip.

Сайнуу
Hello

миний ачааны машин эвдэрсэн
My truck has broken down

Zofia knew how lucky she was that these experts would be guiding them through their country and into the desert, and she could only hope they would be able to offer something in return.

The winter passed and soon it was time for Zofia to leave. With a head full of facts, and a heart full of excitement, she boarded the plane that would carry her, finally, to the desert.

She was standing in the capital city of Ulaanbaatar, her skin burning under the clear sky and her throat sore from the dry, thin air. She was soon to begin the long, difficult journey to the Nemegt Valley and Tsaagan Khushuu, and then north to Bayanzag, the graveyard of the dinosaurs.

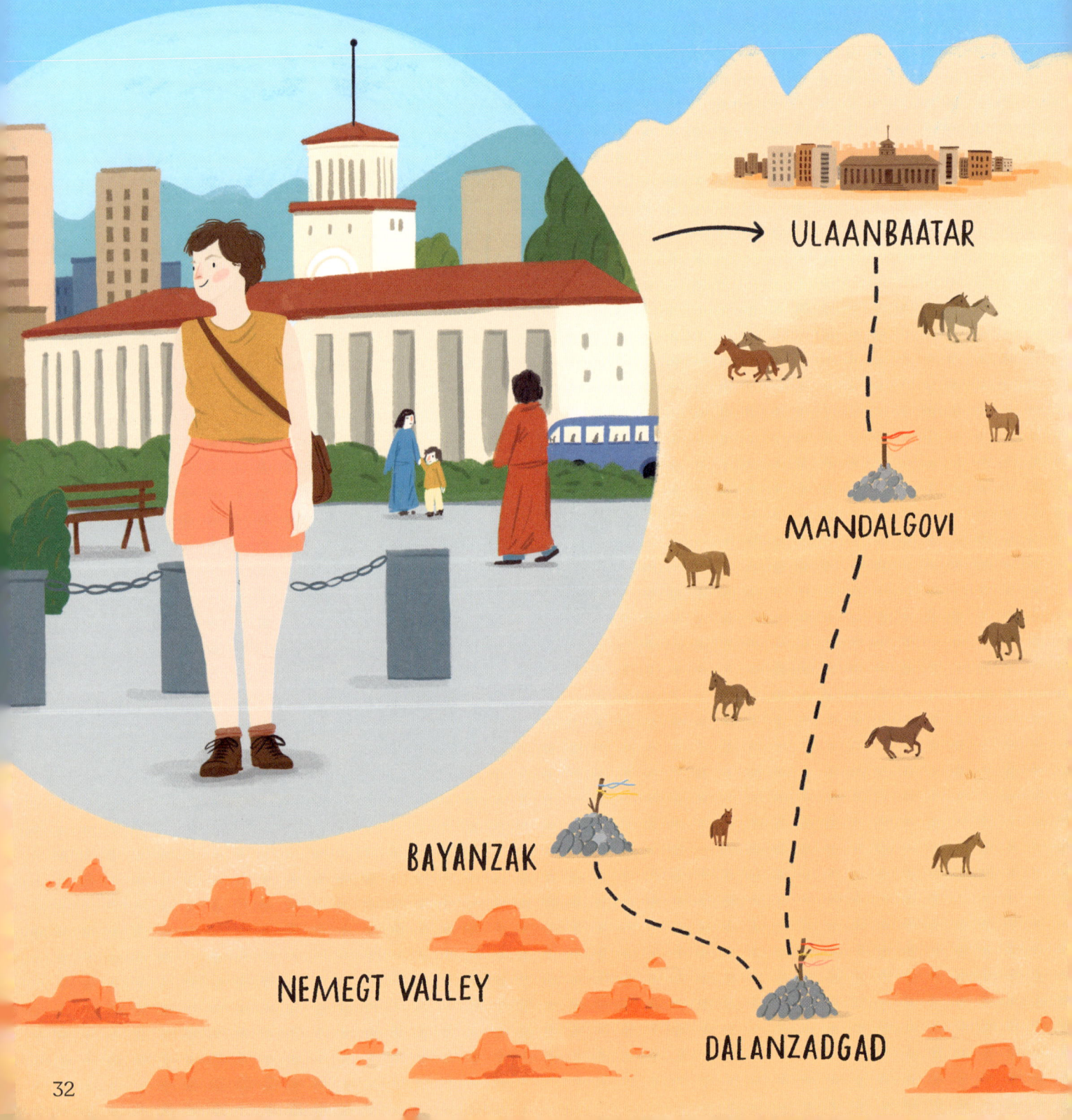

ULAANBAATAR

MANDALGOVI

BAYANZAK

NEMEGT VALLEY

DALANZADGAD

Alone, in a world unknown to her, she should have been lost. But joining her was Mr Dagva, from the Mongolian Academy of Sciences. He spoke Polish beautifully and could help direct their driver, Batochir, who raced through the steppe, somehow picking out the invisible 1,000km route, while singing folk songs from behind the wheel.

Beneath the endless sky, the ground seemed to go on forever, broken only by occasional *ovoo* mounds – ancient signposts that once showed silk-road travellers the routes home. They passed camels and horses, but no people.

After 48 hours, they reached Dalanzadgad and rested in a park at the centre of the small town – a shining oasis within the endless desert – before driving another 300km to Bayanzag, cold and high on the steppe. But that night, Zofia would spend her first night in a *ger*.

The next day, Zofia, Mr Dagva and Batochir met the rest of the team who had set up camp in Naranbulag, sheltered by a dune overgrown with tamarisk shrubs, in the southern part of the Nemegt Valley.

Jerzy Lefeld
geologist

Jerzy Małecki
palaeontologist

Zofia Kielan-Jaworowska
palaeontologist

Józef Kaźmierczak
palaeontologist

Andrzej Sulimski
palaeontologist

Namsrai
lab assistant

Galsan
lab assistant

Khosbayar
geologist

Teresa Maryańska
palaeontologist: expert on armoured dinosaurs

Ryszard Gradziński
chief geologist

Halszka Osmólska
palaeontologist: expert in therapods

Edmund Rachtan
palaeontologist

Gwidon Jakubowski
palaeontologist

Wojciech Skarżyński
technical assista and sculptor

In Mongolia, people used to have just one name. It was only after the 1990s that many started using both a first and last name.

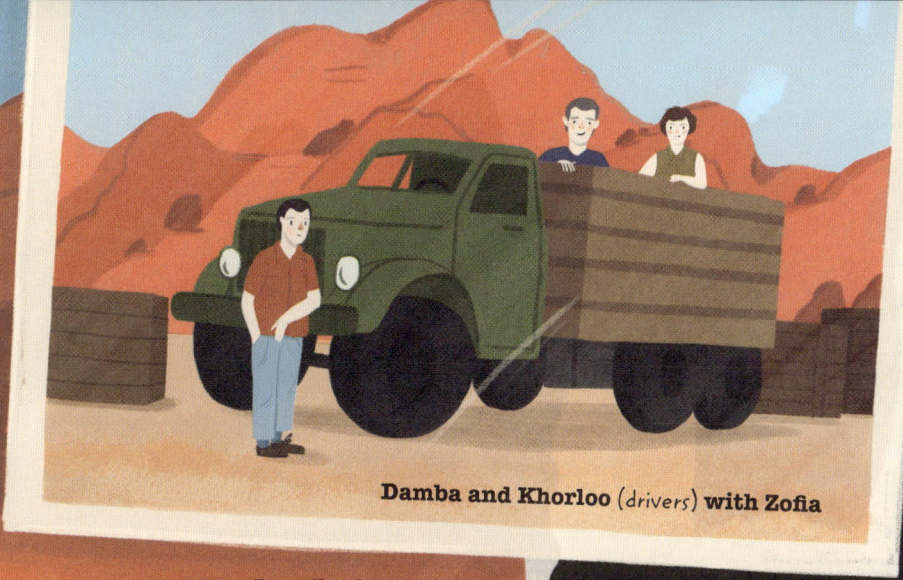

Damba and Khorloo (drivers) with Zofia

Erdenebulgan
technical assistant

Khaltar
technical assistant

Lam Dzal
senior labourer

Zofia had assembled an amazing team of young adventurers, and they were joined by an equally brilliant group of Mongolian scientists. As no one from Zofia's Polish team had seen the desert before, they watched and listened to their new Mongolian friends, learning how to survive in this new – but ancient – world.

Henryk Kubiak
palaeontologist: expert in fossil elephants and rhinos

Demberel Dashzeveg
palaeontologist: expert on mammals

Naidan Dovchin
palaeontologist

Rinchen Barsbold
palaeontologist: expert on dinosaurs

The valley ran for over 160km from east to west through the Gobi Desert and formed a split in the Earth. It was here they hoped to discover the animals, preserved since the Cretaceous, in the sandy rocks.

A DAY IN THE LIFE OF THE DESERT CAMP

Life in the camp was not going to be a holiday. They woke at seven each morning after a freezing night, the frost on their tents crackling as they unzipped the doors.

After a speedy breakfast of Mongolian tea boiled in milk they set off on their work.

Moving slowly across the dusty ground, their eyes close to the sand, they 'prospected' for fossils. No matter what they found, they would have to stop by lunchtime when the temperatures rose to over 40°C. Forced into the shade, they returned to their work in the late afternoon until the light began to fail.

Each night as the sun set, they discussed what they had prised from the sandy rocks. They would build a fire from the paper-dry desert shrubs, which grew around their camp, to boil water and cook the canned food they had shipped from Europe.

There was no tap for fresh water, and any rain they collected quickly evaporated (sometimes before it even hit the ground). Instead, all their water for cooking, drinking, washing, and cooling their trucks had to be collected from a well 40km away – so everyone was only allowed to drink a few cups per day.

In the light of their evening fires, they were surrounded by clouds of biting insects so thick that they had to sit down to their evening meals with their heads and faces wrapped in scarves.

They made the most of it – laughing at how silly they looked, singing songs to raise their spirits and drinking *Khoormog* (fermented camel milk) that their Mongolian friends shared with them.

Despite their laughter, working in the camp could be dangerous. Mongolia was five times the size of Poland but home to fewer people than lived in the whole of Warsaw. With no one to ask directions from and no radio communications, if they got lost, they might never find their way back.

But Zofia and her team were not alone in the Gobi. Beside them as they worked were the desert's non-human inhabitants…

Gobi jerboas (*Allactaga bullata*)
These nocturnal mammals avoided the devastating temperatures by burrowing under the ground during the day.

Gobi pit vipers (*Gloydius halys*)
Like all pit vipers, this snake, difficult to see against the brown sands and rocks of the desert, was venomous. Although some members of the team thought these snakes should be destroyed, Wojciech preferred picking them up by their tail and carrying them to safety far away.

Zofia had to look out for scorpions and spiders to avoid stings or bites, but a far greater danger could descend from the skies: it wasn't long before she lived through her first sandstorm.

She had been working inside her tent when she saw a grey thunder cloud. Within minutes, the breeze grew faster and stronger, until their tent ropes snapped and their equipment scattered. A tower of speeding sand blotted the sun from the sky and in near darkness Zofia and her team threw themselves on top of their tents, holding them down while the sand whipped their skin and tore at their eyes.

Gobi scorpions
(*Mesobuthus eupeus*)
Although not deadly, the venomous strike of a scorpion's sting was extremely painful!

Camel-spiders (*Solifugids*)
Fast, aggressive and armed with powerful jaws, these arachnids appear to be a mix of spider and scorpion – no one wanted to find one of these in their sleeping bags!

Long-eared hedgehogs
(*Hemiechinus auritus*)
Like many other desert-dwelling mammals, this hedgehog's ears were very long to help it draw heat away from its body. These hedgehogs had a habit of raiding the expedition's rubbish, making a mess in the process.

Tarvaga marmots (*Marmota sibirica*)
Despite their cuteness, everyone tried their best to stay away from these rodents, as they could carry pneumonic plague – a deadly disease for humans.

Sandstorms could last longer than an hour and, after the wind had calmed, the camp always looked like a battle site and would take days to be repaired.

Soon all the hardship began to pay off.

Zofia and Gwidon discovered the fossilised skull of a dinosaur: its tell-tale snout, its eye sockets, the shape of its teeth, all revealed the story of its ancestry.

Slowly and carefully they began to expose the delicate bones - first with spades, picks and chisels, and then with spatulas and eventually paint brushes.

As they gradually removed fragments of stone, the team freed an animal wondrous to behold in its preserved sleep. The slender, powerful skull lay at the end of a curved neck, and they soon discovered ribs, small arms, powerful hips and legs, and a long tail, balancing the weight of the dinosaur's muscles, stomach and head.

After only a few days in the field, they had discovered an almost complete *Tarbosaurus*, a 10m predator, cousin of *Tyrannosaurus rex*, that had hunted prey through the seasonal wetlands before being encased in rock for 70 million years.

As the expedition continued, magnificent fossils appeared day after day, including a gigantic 12-tonne sauropod skeleton, so large it would take two weeks to free it from its sandstone prison.

Discovering dinosaurs was only the first step. After recording and photographing the fossils, there remained the enormous task of protecting the remains in plaster and shipping them back to Ulaanbaatar to be studied in the museum.

After a skeleton was found, a wooden frame was built around it and plaster poured in on top of the fossil. After leaving the plaster overnight to harden, a lid was nailed on the crate and a trench dug around the base.

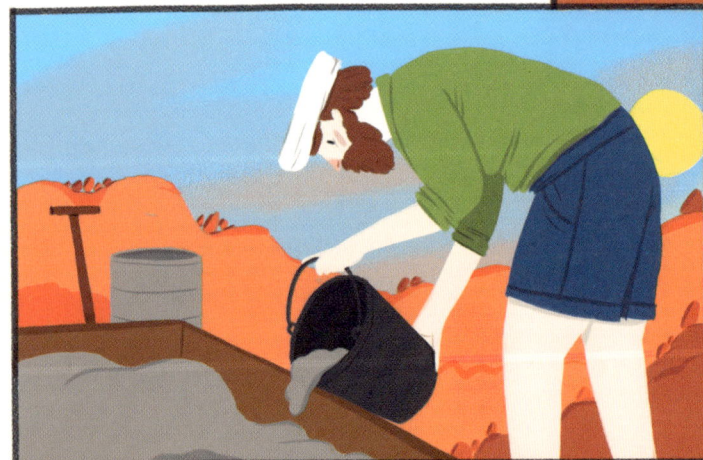

Then, after rope had been attached to the corners, all members of the expedition would pull or push the crate until the rocky stem it sat on cracked and the fossil, safe in its protective casing, snapped off.

When skeletons were spotted in a place too difficult for the trucks to get close to, the dinosaurs had to be cracked from the ground and transported by foot (either being carried or pulled on metal sledges) to wherever the trucks could reach. Freed from their rocky bed, the fossils then sped off to their final destinations, safely bouncing along on the hidden roads.

Zofia's first expedition was a fantastic success. She had led an international group of scientists into the heart of the desert, and despite the heat of the day, the cold of the night, and the back-breaking hard work, they had pulled wonders from the Earth that had been held secret for 70 million years.

But one adventure wasn't enough and over the next seven years, Zofia and her team returned to the Gobi five more times, exploring more of the desert, expanding their gateway to the Cretaceous. Each time they faced new challenges, but every year their amazing discoveries made it worth the sandstorms, sunburns and scorpion stings.

o ULAANBAATAR

MONGOLIA

Nemegt Basin

ALTAN UUL

1. Tsagaan Khushuu (South Nemegt)

Transporting the fossils was not always easy...

You never knew what you might find.

Some of the dinosaurs they discovered were enormous, but others were much smaller, like *Homalocephale* (a tiny relative of the dome-headed *Pachycephalosaurus*) that Zofia found when she turned over an interesting-looking block of stone, only to see a couple of eye sockets looking back at her!

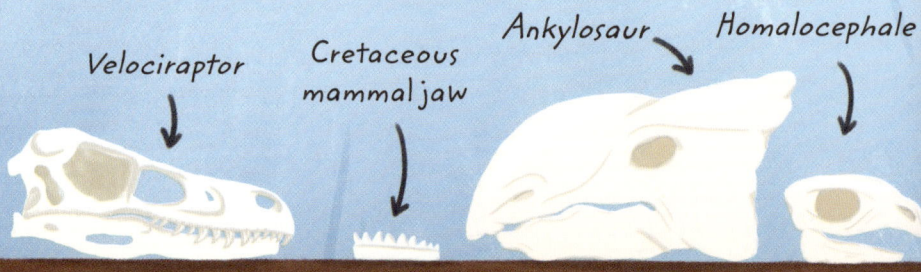

Velociraptor

Cretaceous mammal jaw

Ankylosaur

Homalocephale

An amazing discovery, but difficult to reach!

FOSSIL DISCOVERIES

1. Tsagaan Khushuu (South Nemegt)
The fast-running *Gallimimus*, an ostrich-like dinosaur, was discovered at this site. Its bones were later found to be highly radioactive due to uranium-rich groundwater!

2. Bayanzag
Nine beautifully preserved skulls of Cretaceous mammals were found here, providing important clues about the evolution of our furry ancestors.

3. Khulsan
An unknown ankylosaur was discovered within the basin. Difficult to reach, the team needed scaffolding to scale the cliff side.

4. Tugrugiin Shiree
In 1971, Teresa Maryańska and the team discovered a *Velociraptor* and *Protoceratops* fossilised as if in battle. Did they die fighting or was the *Velociraptor* scavenging for a meal?

- 4. Tugrugiin Shiree
- 2. Bayanzag
- BULGAN VILLAGE
  POST OFFICE
- DALANZADGAD
- 3. Khulsan

Gallimimus

BULGAN VILLAGE
The only post office for hundreds of kilometres.

ALTAN UUL
'The Café' at Altan uul was close to the Polish-Mongolian camps.

DALANZADGAD
The capital of the southern Gobi province where food and tools were stored.

It was in Altan uul that Zofia would make one of her greatest discoveries...

It was the Festival of Naadam – the Mongolian national holiday – and everyone was celebrating.

Folk songs had been sung around the campfire, while they ate *argali* with rice washed down with lots of cups of *Khoormog*. Chief geologist Ryszard had stunned everyone by walking barefoot over the hot coals of the fire.

It had been a wonderful change of their routine, but the next day would be even more unusual. It was, for one thing, raining.

Rain in the Gobi was very rare and Zofia didn't think she would have much luck spotting anything in the darkened, soaked sand.

But soon she was stopped in her tracks as, lying in front of her, half-exposed to the overcast sky, stretched a collection of thin bones. As she started to clear the sand from the fossils, she couldn't believe her eyes. She had found an arm, a hand, and then a 20cm-long curved claw...

Back at the camp, no one quite believed her when she described what she had found. This was no tiny-armed *Tarbosaurus*. This was enormous. This was… what was this?

The next day, with Edmund's, Halszka's, and Rinchen's help, she found more: a shoulder bone longer than she was tall, and an arm 2.4m long, tipped with three knife-like claws.

After a dusty day of excitement and confusion, Halszka, Teresa, Henryk and Zofia tore through the expedition's library, but none of their books helped at all.

With claws like that, imagine its monstrous teeth!

What did it eat?

Was this a new form of predator?

How large was it?

Zofia's dinosaur arm wasn't just unusual, they didn't even know what sort of dinosaur it was from.

On that rainy morning, Zofia had stumbled upon what would become one of the greatest mysteries of palaeontology in the 20th century…

This terrifying fossil would be named *Deinocheirus* meaning 'horrible hand' but they had no idea who the arms had belonged to. In fact, the whole world would have to wait almost 50 years for the rest of the dinosaur's skeleton to be discovered…

Tarchia

Deinocheirus' stupendous arms were attached to an almost unbelievable animal. Standing at almost the same height as *Tyrannosaurus rex* and at 11m long, it was an 'ostrich-like dinosaur' so large it probably couldn't run.

It was a theropod (a member of the same group of dinosaurs as *T. rex*, *Velociraptor* and *Allosaurus*) but it had no teeth in its wide metre-long duck-like beak. A sickle-clawed giant with a pot-belly and, probably, a glorious covering of feathers descending over a towering humped back.

Deinocheirus

Alioramus

Its vast claws would have helped it draw down branches to eat or scoop huge quantities of soft aquatic plants from the streams of freshwater it waded through. Its shovel-like mouth would munch the plants down into its enormous stomach, where stones it had swallowed helped smash up the hard-to-digest greens.

Deinocheirus was an omnivore, swallowing the occasional fish along with its water-salads, but this was the extent of its meat-eating. Its 'horrible hands' were the dinosaur's cutlery, not the devastating weapons decades of palaeontologists thought they must have been.

At the end of each expedition, the fossils, safe in their plaster cocoons, were divided between the Mongolian and Polish teams. The Polish collection travelled by train to Warsaw, and the remaining fossils stayed in Ulaanbaatar to be studied by Demberel, Naidan, Rinchen and their students.

Saurolophus
Found: Nemegt Basin
Size: 13m long
Species description: Large duck-billed herbivore

Gallimimus
Found: Tsaagan Khushuu
Size: 6m long
Species description: Fast-running, probably omnivorous.

Opisthocoelicaudia (reconstruction)
Found: Altan uul
Size: 12m long
Species description: Herbivorous sauropod

Prenocephale
Found: Khulsan and Nemegt
Size: 2m long
Species description: Bipedal herbivore

Nemegtosaurus (skull)
Found: Nemegt Basin
Size: Unknown
Species description: Herbivorous sauropod

It took years to remove the last of the desert rock from the fossilised bones, until finally it was time to hoist them up and show everyone what they had discovered. In 1968 at the Palace of Culture, dinosaurs from the Gobi Desert astonished the people of Warsaw.

Deinocheirus
Found: Altan uul
Size: 11m long (when finally discovered)
Species description: (unknown until 21st century)

Wide-eyed children squealed beneath the awe-inspiring grin of *Tarbosaurus* and the extraordinary might of *Opisthocoelicaudia*, while their parents pondered on the mysterious arms of *Deinocheirus* and the wonderful remains of *Protoceratops*.

Saichania
Found: Khulsan
Size: 7m long
Species description: Medium-sized, heavily armoured herbivore

Tarbosaurus
Found: Nemegt Basin
Size: 10m long
Species description: Carnivorous tyrannosaurid

But Zofia wasn't looking at the dinosaurs – *she had other animals on her mind.*

Protoceratops
Found: Bayanzag
Size: 2.5m long
Species description: Herbivorous ceratopsian

Ever since she had first seen drawings of *Deltatheridium* and *Zalambdalestes* in Professor Kozłowski's apartment, Zofia had dreamed of discovering mammals from the age of the dinosaurs.

But the pursuit of early mammals was no picnic. Dinosaur fossils were often much larger than the humans digging them up, whereas ancient mammals had tiny, fragile bones that often broke away from their skeletons. Zofia would spend hours on her stomach, her face close to the ground, looking for millimetre-long teeth glinting in the sunlight or fingernail-long jaw bones.

Before her first expedition, only 11 mammal skulls from the Cretaceous period had ever been found but, by the end of 1965, Zofia and her team had almost doubled that number, just from Bayanzag!

Kennalestes skull

On one expedition, Zofia took her team to the dark-red rocks of Hermiin Tsav where they quickly began finding mammals thanks to their slow, steady, head-down approach. Then, when exploring Khulsan, they struck scientific gold. No human had ever before seen the animals they were to discover, and these fossils would help change how the world thought about the first mammals...

Zofia was fascinated by these *multituberculates* and would spend the next fifty years studying them. After first evolving during the age of *Diplodocus* and *Stegosaurus* in the Jurassic period, they had bloomed by the Cretaceous into the most common and varied mammals on Earth.

Nemegtosaurus

Opisthocoelicaudia

Shuvuuia

Catopsbaatar

Saichania

Taeniolabis

Kryptobaatar

Nemegtbaatar

Alioramus

They burrowed beneath the feet of *Velociraptor*, hopped on two legs away from the snapping jaws of *Shuvuuia*, and clung to branches above the head of *Alioramus*.

Velociraptor

Kennalestes

Chulsanbaatar

These creatures didn't live in the shadows of the dinosaurs, but were a fascinating branch on the tree of life that bred and battled, hunted and flourished, surviving for a further thirty million years after the dinosaurs disappeared.

Zofia had spent eight summers in the Gobi and it was now a 'home away from home'. She recognised faces everywhere she went and places that had once sounded mysterious – Bayanzag, Altan uul, Dalanzadgad – were now as familiar to her as the streets of Warsaw.

Zofia and her team had once been the only humans in the desert for hundreds of kilometres around, but each summer more and more people arrived, eager to uncover treasures of their own. The competition for resources grew fierce, and with their expeditions already uncovering more fossils than they had ever imagined, it was time to move on.

So, sadly, in 1971, after years of working together, Zofia and her team finally waved goodbye to their friends as they travelled back to Poland. Sunburnt and sad to be leaving, Zofia cradled the collection of mammal fossils they had uncovered together – the greatest collection ever to have been discovered from the age of the dinosaurs.

Zofia returned to the concrete and drizzle of Warsaw but also the warmth of her family. Although she was home, she never truly left the desert where she and her friends had made their discoveries.

To celebrate their finds, Zofia and the expeditions' technician Wojciech Skarżyński recreated life-size constructions at the Silesian Zoological Park in Chorzów for everyone to enjoy!

The Dinosaur Valley was completed in 1974 with seven Mongolian species: *Tarbosaurus*, *Nemegtosaurus*, *Saurolophus*, *Protoceratops*, *Saichania*, *Prenocephale* and *Gallimimus*.

Zofia wrote books about her expeditions and appeared on TV (sneaking dinosaur eggs into the studios in her handbag), talking about the wonders of the natural world.

In labs, she tried to make sense of the rocky fossil puzzles from the Gobi Desert, alongside young students who were as captivated by her stories of adventures as she had been listening to the tales of Roy Chapman Andrews in her war-torn youth.

ZOFIA KIELAN-JAWOROWSKA

And despite the war, Zofia connected with people - no matter who they were, where they lived, what language they spoke or what they believed in - through the shared joy of discovery. She uncovered the secrets of a world before ghettos, iron curtains or cold wars. Recognising that science cannot be done in isolation, she made sure her work travelled outward across nations, uniting us in our shared history on this planet…

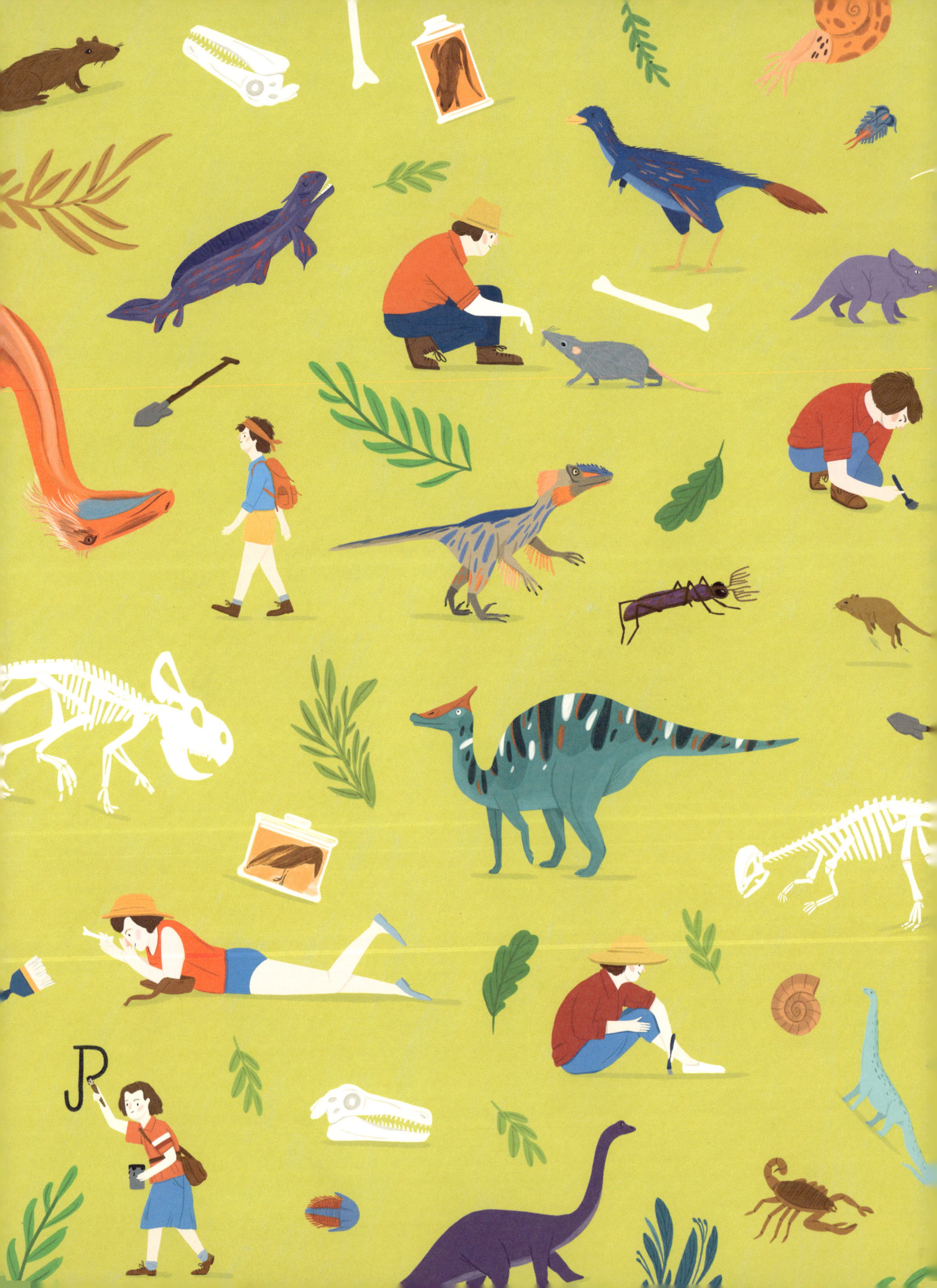
JR